The Farm Wife's Almanac

THE DREAMSEEKER
POETRY SERIES

Books in the DreamSeeker Poetry Series, intended to make available fine writing by Anabaptist-related poets, are published by Cascadia Publishing House under the DreamSeeker Books imprint and often copublished with Herald Press. Cascadia oversees content of these poetry collections in collaboration with the DreamSeeker Poetry Series Editor Jeff Gundy (Jean Janzen volumes 1-4) as well as when called for in consultation with its Editorial Council and the authors themselves.

Also worth noting are two poetry collections that would likely have been included in the series had it been in existence then:

DreamSeeker Books also continues to release occasional high-caliber collections of poems outside of the DreamSeeker Poetry Series:

The Farm Wife's Almanac

Poems by

Shari Wagner

DreamSeeker Poetry Series, Volume 16

DreamSeeker Books
TELFORD, PENNSYLVANIA

an imprint of
Cascadia Publishing House LLC

Cascadia Publishing House orders, information, reprint permissions:
contact@CascadiaPublishingHouse.com
1-215-723-9125
126 Klingerman Road, Telford PA 18969
www.CascadiaPublishingHouse.com

DreamSeeker Books is an imprint of Cascadia Publishing House LLC
ISBN 13: 978-1-68027-015-0 ISBN 10: 1-68027-015-X
Book design by Cascadia Publishing House
Cover design by Gwen M. Stamm
Cover painting, "Full Moon Winter Haiku,"
copyright © by John J. Domont

Versions of poems in this collection have appeared in various outlets. For a complete listing, see Acknowledgments section, back of book.

Library of Congress Cataloguing-in-Publication Data
Names: Wagner, Shari, 1958- author.
Title: The farm wife's almanac / poems by Shari Wagner.
Description: Telford, Pennsylvania : DreamSeeker Books, 2019. | Series:
  Dreamseeker Poetry Series ; volume 16
Identifiers: LCCN 2019001974| ISBN 9781680270150 (trade pbk. : alk.
paper) |
  ISBN 168027015X (trade pbk. : alk. paper)
Classification: LCC PS3623.A3564 A6 2019 | DDC 811/.6--dc23
LC record available at https://lccn.loc.gov/2019001974

24 23 22 21 20 19   10 9 8 7 6 5 4 3 2 1

For Doris Jean Mast
Beloved aunt and farm wife extraordinaire

CONTENTS

Proverbs & Parables

Oddities

Tidal Chart

Pastimes

Travel

Whoever doesn't respect the little bit isn't worthy of the whole.
—Mennonite Proverb

The
Farm Wife's
Almanac

The farm wife predicts the weather

Mom taught me, like her mother taught her,
to look for cats sneezing, crows prancing,

poplars turning over their leaves. Observing
the signs takes us back to the first farm wife

reckoning a harsh winter from the tough
rind of an apple. After the flood, Noah's wife

put two and two together: *Harm a barn swallow,*
and it will rain for a month. I add to my almanac

Matthew 16: *Red sky at night, sailors' delight.*
Red sky in morning, sailors take warning.

Mary knew her son would need a sign
of wind and thunder. My daughters trust

their phones. Go outside, I tell them.
Songbirds are silent. The crow flies alone.

In the Garden

The farm wife sings to the snake in her garden

"Be Thou My Vision"
I hum so you know

I am coming to pluck
green beans in the dark

where you dangle.
O garter snake,

you are the refrain
that returns after every verse

I sing. I spy you
in the melon's ropey vine

or the smooth handle
of a hoe half-hidden

in marigolds. Against
the picket fence,

your discarded skin
hangs thin as tissue

paper once wrapped
around a gift.

The farm wife examines her Mennonite roots

They're the riddle in my garden:
    "What has eyes but cannot see?"
Like a stone, they fit my hand
    as I turn their other cheek.
With love but no regrets,
    I mash them into mounds
or whip them, scallop them,
    dice them for rivel soup.
Cancer could not lessen
    Dad's affection for them fried.
He tells how they clustered
    like sleigh bells in the sand
where nothing else but winter
    squash and zucchini thrived.
His mother, Fannie Mishler,
    fixed them for every meal,
paring as she would visit,
    the way some women knit.
My son-in-law from St. Louis
    splashes hot sauce on their skin,
but I fancy even their faces,
    pockmarked or sliced by the
shovel, that shrivel as they age.

The farm wife describes meeting her husband at a "walk-a-mile"—a Mennonite dating game

The last light was touching the tassels
when the quiet boy from Emma Church

tapped the guy with his eye on college
and told him to move forward five couples.

That's how I met Pete. From the soft way
he scuffed the gravel and whistled

to a red-winged blackbird, I knew
he wasn't the sort to shoot the starlings

or tell me how to keep my house.
Not like the boys who talked to be talking

and walked so close they almost pushed me
in the ditch. When Lu Miller told me,

"Move back nine," I did with regret
but tagged her back when the next girl said,

"Go forward four," and I added five.
It was cheating, but that's how you knew

someone liked you—when they came back.
At Fly Creek, cicadas were clicking

and swallows brushed the darkness
with their wings. Or maybe they were bats.

Pete and I dropped back and stood at the railing
to hear the frogs. It was dark enough

he could ask if I had plans for next evening
and I slid my hand in his. Our grandkids laugh

when I say they should walk-a-mile.
When they like someone, they text

and call that dating, though they might be
a hundred miles apart.

The farm wife eats out at Marner's Six Mile Café

Widowed farmers cram the table
near the peanut butter pies,

but I prefer the back booth
beneath a pike framed with flowers.

Under a coffee cup's "Start your day
with Jesus," I find Topeka Seed & Stove.

Once, when it was crowded,
we ate in the kitchen where an Amish cook

beat the batter while flipping eggs
and watching toast. Annie doesn't bring

us menus. She knows the grandkids and I
will order pancakes with cinnamon butter

faces. When my sisters visit, they say,
"Let's go someplace with atmosphere."

They mean a chain near the interstate
where they decorate with sport stars

and license plates, where the booths
are so tall, you can't see your neighbors.

The farm wife shares her view on windows in the new sanctuary

Some members are voting for clear glass
while others believe frosted would be nicer.

I prefer a view of Ed Troyer's cows
and a way to survey the sky. It gives me pause

to think of everyone in the same room
with no way to look out and no sunlight

crossing the pews. Call the outside a distraction,
but I'd rather pray with the Amish in a barn,

the big door flung open and swallows with forked
tails, darting in and out. I'm saying this softly

because even Mennonites who favor clear glass
might see some taint of worldliness, unsettling

as the stained glass in the old sanctuary
when it was Methodist. Sam Troyer, Ed's father,

loaded those windows on a wagon headed
for the dump, but he took a wrong turn. Now

no one in LaGrange County has a prettier
barn than Ed's. You should see the milking parlor,

how lilies of the field hold the light.

The farm wife turns off the TV evangelist

The Jesus I grew up with
likes to be outside.
If he's not fishing, he's picking figs
or showing us his mustard crop.

He prefers dusty roads, the common sparrow,
and lilies of the field.
When he knocks on your door
holding a lantern, you know it's time
to buckle on overshoes
and go with him to feed the sheep.

But this preacher, who looks straight
into the camera and claims he knows
Jesus, says what he wants
is for me to believe in him
so he can come inside.

That sounds shifty to me.
Like a wolf with his paws dipped in flour.

Jesus who heals the blind
said we will know a tree by its fruit.

The farm wife argues with God in the garden

I'm on my knees in the strawberry patch
when I start the argument: Why did you prefer

Abel's lamb to Cain's fresh greens
and corn on the cob slathered in butter?

Was it the smoke curling up to heaven
you desired? There's plenty of steam

in my kitchen when I'm canning.
Or was it the tune Abel played on his flute?

There's nothing prettier than the plink
of jar lids as they're sealing. Cain could've used

your thumbs up to help him grasp his hoe
and wield the axe. We farmers kill the rooster,

too, you know, and butcher steers.
But it's not something we talk about.

There's more pleasure in paring potatoes
or shelling pods. If it's the sacrifice of a life

you want—I'd say there's life in these bull
thistles, and beauty, too, persistence in how

they sprout back with deeper roots.
If it's blood that calls you—why not what

comes with the cycle of the moon?
Or the sweetness of the watermelon, split open,

all that red juice on your mouth and hands.

The farm wife repeats a lullaby

When Ruth cried out, terrified
by what stalked the root cellar

or chased her toward a cliff,
we sang our favorite chorus:

Vegetables grow in my garden,
God sends the rain.

Vegetables grow in my garden,
God sends the sun.

With each verse, we substituted
something new: *carrots, potatoes,*

rutabagas, coconuts. Like sheep
that leap a fence, we never stopped

to reconsider: *sunflowers,*
snapdragons, poinsettia, burr

thistle. Rabbits wriggled in
and soon the gate swung open

for *rhinoceros* and *pythons* . . .
till we made room for everything

under the sun, under the rain.

Recipes & Remedies

The farm wife lists the top ten virtues she keeps by hanging laundry outside

Trust. Because everything hinges on the weather
    and a breeze whipping out the wrinkles.

Honesty. Because it's all out there for neighbors to see.

Discretion. Because some things, nevertheless,
    should be hung toward the house.

Thrift. Because each pin doubles up to hold two sleeves.

Gratitude. Because the sun is a natural bleach.

Diligence. Because the up and down keeps me on my toes.

Patience. Because I wrestle with the wind.

Humility. Because I do it barefoot.

Faith. Because sheets smell of sunshine in December.

Tenderness. Because frozen overalls stand up
    though no one is inside.

The farm wife hoists the family flag

Eve trudged off the bus in tears the day
her third-grade teacher scolded her
for using a hankie. "It's not sanitary," she said.
Miss Pauley had no notion of what
a handkerchief means to us: reusable tissue,
wash cloth, gripper of lids, wiper of smudgy
glasses, emergency bandage, keepsake

we carry to the grave. Peekaboo with a hankie
triggered Eve's first laugh, and later she sat
through sermons watching Grandma Yoder
fold a flat square into a butterfly or mouse.
Eve did that for her sisters and knotted Ruth's
Sunday pennies in a corner like a hobo's sack.
She ironed and stacked all the hankies

in our drawers and brought a bandanna drenched
with cold water to her dad who tied it round
his neck. Last Christmas she gave me a set
of four lacy kerchiefs embroidered by her own
hand, each with my initials and a leaf or flower
to signify the season. Straight from a city college,
Miss Pauley could only count the virtues

of Kleenex. "Like a lot of things, hankies grow
softer with age," I said, using one to wipe Eve's tears.

The farm wife posts on her fridge

"You need to get on Facebook," my sisters
tell me, but this space keeps me plenty busy,
posting with veggie magnets I never have
enough of. A turkey that fits my grandson's
first-grade hand straddles a postcard of
Sunny Sarasota and a prayer card from
church. The grocery list I forgot to take
secures the electric bill we need to pay.
"You need to clear this off," Pete complains
when he opens the door and another photo
flutters to the floor. Sometimes I do remove
clippings from *The Budget,* old obituaries,
and invitations to haystack suppers. But it's
tricky to choose when one post fortifies
another. Yesterday's hymn sing holds a note
from sewing circle that pins a belated birthday
blessing on a faded valentine.

The farm wife reveals her recipe for letters

I keep each one going for days
like Amish friendship bread, adding more

of this, a little of that, to fill both sides
of a page in blue, green, black, or pencil.

My sisters prefer to telephone or text.
They wonder how I find so much to write,

but each installment starts with the sun,
how much rain has fallen, how tall the corn.

Then I note what's in the oven. Margins
overflow with ham and mashed potatoes,

green bean casserole, creamy cucumber
and onion salad. One thought leads

to another like warm peach cobbler or cups
of coffee passed around the table. Ideas

slip through a gap in the garden fence—
I herd them back before I forget

and begin to hang the wash or count
new quarts of stewed tomatoes.

Company comes, company goes.
The corn is down to stubble. I add

three feet of snow, a full bucket of
Plymouth Rock eggs, and with the raising

of a red flag, send out my thick epistles.
But who has time to write back?

Not even my pen pal in prison.

The farm wife finds her necklace in the junk drawer

That's what's left of it—
    six safety pins
from a chain I once wore
    beneath my dress to Saylor's
School and Forks Mennonite
    Church. Who'd suspect
vanity in a girl so shy
    she seldom spoke? I liked
how each pin clicked shut
    to link to the next
and how they encircled me
    like a charm of daisies
I counted round and
    round. Some would have said
that was a sin. The same
    folks who'd pocket a shiny
buckeye against the ache
    of rheumatism.
I took my necklace off
    when I joined my life
with Pete's. I needed pins
    for diapers, school notes,
lost buttons, loose straps—
    catastrophes
only the quick clasp
    of hidden silver fixed.

The farm wife feels the pinch of her inheritance

Grandma Fannie called it "simplicity of spirit"
when she warmed the breakfast dishwater
for lunch and told us not to flush because

once a day was sufficient. When Grandpa
had to *go,* she sent him to irrigate tomatoes.
To entertain us, she passed shoeboxes

of old postcards from Sarasota, greetings
from the dead. On my mom's side, Grandma Iva
wrote her letters in tiny script, pressed

to the edge to get her money's worth.
Iva's husband, Grandpa Milt, was so tight
he reeked of peppermint oil, his remedy

for any ailment. Mom, herself, spent hours
in any store, turning her back and then returning,
drawn to what was forbidden but delicious.

If she bought a coin purse, for penance we ate
cornbread soaked in milk. I know her dance—forward
and back. I step into her hand-me-down

shoes and cook my rivel soup. What begins
in simplicity wants to claim my house.
Are the plastic bags I wash and save

a gift to the earth or my inheritance jamming
the drawers? If only I could hold my arms open
to take in and let go—like the scarecrow

I made from a bag of rags.

The farm wife gives us her recipe for rivel soup

It's so simple, I carry it in my head:
peel 2 or 3 potatoes and dice them
with green onion. Cook till soft enough
to mash, then pour in several quarts of milk,
but don't throw out the water. In a bowl,
stir one egg with ½ cup flour. Keep stirring
with a fork and shaking in more flour
till rivels the size of your smallest fingernail
form. When the milk with potato water
begins to boil, add rivels with one hand
while stirring with the other. Don't stop
or you'll scorch the pan, but don't hurry.
My first time, I sprinkled too quickly
and rivels collected in a ball, big as a fist.
My thrifty mother cooked this as repentance
when she'd return from shopping. The secret,
she said, was rubbing the dumplings
between her thumb and index finger.
But if you don't want rivels under your nails,
use a fork. Cook and stir till they're chewy—
5 or 10 minutes, though I never watch the clock.
Season with salt and pepper. Add celery
seed to be fancy. We eat this in winter
with cheese and homemade bread.

The farm wife ponders her mother's cookbook

I cook by heart, adding more of this, less
of that, but Mom, bless her soul, never strayed
from *The Mennonite Community Cookbook.*

Among the pages, I find slick pamphlets
she picked up at church: *Golden Hours
with the Bible*, *The Most Costly Gift*,

Where Will You Be Five Minutes After You Die?
No wonder she complained of insomnia.
She never wrote "delicious" or "wonderful"

in the margins, only the same refrain: "Tried"
and "Tried." But I can tell she favored
something sweet by where the spatters fell.

The farm wife marvels at her mother's ordered house

The doe fastened to her fawns
with dainty chains stood for sixty years
near the creamer in the china closet.

Knives, spoons, and forks never fraternized,
the way they do in my drawer.
Dominoes was Mom's game—

lining up the dots and blanks. At night,
when my sisters and I whispered
beneath the stitches of her double-ringed

quilts, we heard the creak of tired footsteps
and then her voice: "Girls, it's time to sleep."
As if there was a time for silence and time

enough for laughter, as if the sun was inside
the first egg she broke each morning.

The farm wife makes her Christmas list

Give me sisters and brothers with crockpots full
and running over. A bed piled high with coats

and diaper bags. Leaves to extend the kitchen table.
Thick catalogs to booster seat the kids.

A percolator perking thirty cups as we pass
plates of monster cookies and whoopee pies.

Albums with ancestors solid as their barns.
Battered Rook cards we use to shoot the moon

and dominoes branching in every direction.
Paper snowflakes till strings of hearts

replace them. The old piano we can't afford
to tune, that gives us our pitch when we sing

"Praise God from Whom All Blessings Flow,"
the version with echoing alleluias and amens.

Silence washing over us as we wave to the last
car pulling out, side by side like newlyweds.

Proverbs & Parables

The farm wife leafs through Iva's Bible

On Sunday mornings, Grandma Iva
slipped me sticks of chewing gum

and used her King James as a base
for creasing the handkerchief

she turned under to release a butterfly.
Proverbs 31 holds that hankie

she embroidered with her own initials
and blue forget-me-nots. Here's a bulletin

where Grandma wrote in secret code:
I C U 8 2 B 4 I 8 1. Look how we squeezed in

a game of dots and boxes while listening
to some stream of a sermon, drier

than the four-leaf clover hidden
in Leviticus. Booklets for the dead

are scattered like mustard seeds
and tucked between the map of Jerusalem

and the Missionary Journeys of Paul
is the glimmer of a gum wrapper,

silver like the origami paper
my granddaughter folds into a crane.

Lord only knows what wonders
would be seen if I shook Iva's Bible

like Eve shook the apple tree.

The farm wife cites Proverbs 31:17—"She girds her loins with strength and makes her arms strong"

My daughters can't get over
how big the women are
in the family photo album.
Ruth describes Grandma Iva
as a lady Goliath, dwarfing
the bearded brethren on either side.

Sarah adds that Grandma Fannie
might be a Viking,
the way she towers on her porch,
wearing her covering
like a horned helmet. Her rolled-up
sleeves reveal thick forearms,
fists clench the handles
of invisible buckets.

"Fannie was a mild woman," I say.

"Are you kidding?" my sister
Neva cuts in. "She carried a switch
and chased children with it.
I remember cleaning her false teeth—
thinking they might bite."

With milkshake diets and jogging,
the women in my family work
hard to slim Holstein hips
and legs stout as Belgian horses.

But even when they starve themselves
into weakness, our inheritance remains
like the framework of a barn
that bows to nothing
but the gravity that would claim it.

The farm wife recounts a close call

At thirteen I decided
no life of sweeping

and pulling weeds for me!
No endless wringer

and clothesline. I'd never
tie on Mom's bib apron.

I'd be a star in sequins,
walking with a spotlight

on a wire. So I climbed
to the barn loft, stuffed

my black stockings
in my shoes, grasped

a broken broom for balance,
and stepped out onto the beam.

One foot then another—
easy as "A, B, C

d'Katz schlaft im schnee"—
till I glanced down

at tiny Shep, napping
with the cats. Static

from a distant station
buzzed inside my head.

I was a dust mote
in the Big Top of space,

numb as a tooth
pulled from my body.

Where would I be
if a barred owl's hoot,

"*Who* cooks for you?
Who cooks for you?"

hadn't called me back
to the broom Grandma used

for fifty years? I felt
the sweep of angels,

ascending and descending,
and then their hands on mine,

all of us gripping that handle
like the rung of a ladder

till I reached the other side.

The farm wife quotes her Grandma Iva

"You can get used to anything.
You can get used to hanging
if you hang long enough."

Grandma learned this when she was eight,
when her mother died and her father left
for Wyoming, never sending
the train fare he promised.

Iva worked for her keep
in a household with fourteen children.
Each morning before dawn,
she brought the cows in for milking
and warmed her bare feet
in the steamy grass where they had lain.

I don't know if she married for love
or to flee the endless clothes she fed
through the wringer, then pinned to the line.
Grandpa Milt was a good man
but so stubborn he drove twenty miles
under the speed limit to show the cops
who was boss. He paid hundreds of dollars
for traffic tickets but didn't have the cash
to buy Grandma a nice dress.

To be fair, she never said she wanted one.
And if she had, it would have been black.
That was the only color she wore to church

after the bishop said the lacework
she added to pillowcases contradicted
Proverbs 31:30: "Charm is deceptive,
and beauty is fleeting. . . ." As he turned
for the door, she tacked on the next verse:
"Honor her for all that her hands have done."

Iva's tongue was honey-sweet and stung
like a bee. When Grandpa was too Scotch
to buy me a penny candy, she said,
"Earn all you can. Save all you can.
Can all you save. And sit on the lid."

And when he talked as if he knew
what he knew, and there was no use
to argue, she'd quietly sing,
Have Thine own way, Lord,
Have Thine own way.

Now that I think on it,
she always got in the last word.
When the radio announcer would croon,
Kalamazoo, direct to you,
she'd add, "Kankakee, direct to me"
and smile as if we had a secret.

**The farm wife digs into her purse to offer advice
with a stick of chewing gum**

It's what you make of things that you're given.

Take that man Wrigley.
He drove to Shipshewana from Chicago
to buy a load of spearmint oil
from Larry Yoder's grandpa.

They were closing the deal when the hired man
rushed through the kitchen door, out
of breath, his face beet red. Oh
Lordy, he had ruined all the spearmint
by pouring in peppermint.

Mint oils were as precious as maple syrup.
It took a field to fill a vat.

Mr. Wrigley knew that.
"I'll buy it anyway," he said,
trusting his luck.

That's the story of Doublemint Gum.

The farm wife tells the story of an aunt
who planted trees

An anchor with "Rest in Peace"
decorates her stone
though she set her heart
upon an ocean that rolled like a windy cornfield,
tossing tassels and dark green leaves.

It could take her breath
and never bring it home again.

When asked if she would marry,
Ella said to the wonderment of family
that he would have to be a sailor,
a man who moved lightly across the water,
setting sails by constellations.

But after years she grew tired
waiting in the fields.
For a time she dressed in black
and then put on her white.

When the vows were said and done,
Ella discovered what she never looked to see:
she had married a farmer who counted
his fortune by the bushel,
by the starlings he shot from the rafters.

For every machine he bought,
she bought another tree,
a quaking aspen

to grow in the circle
stretching around her house.

Whenever a gale came from the North,
she stood against the kitchen screen
and heard the leaves
like rising water.

The farm wife speaks for the quiet in the land

Cows appreciate soft-spoken people.
"Come bossy, come boss,"
Dad said, and his Holstein ladies
stopped chewing and trotted to the barn.

Dad never carried a stick,
and the only time he spoke a harsh word
to a cow was when he was milking
and she'd slap him in the face
with her tail.

He knew what to say
when a cow was glum or bullheaded,
but with people he was tongue-tied.

If you don't talk much, not much
can go wrong. He learned that
his first day at Millersburg School
when the teacher outlawed German,
offering an award
for the student who never spoke it.

Mom said she lost her chance day one,
but Dad won hands down—
he never said a word all year
in any language. Years later,
he proposed to Mom in a letter,
though they lived two miles apart.

When she was mute, with a tube in her throat,
Dad hunkered by her side like a boulder
that would not be moved.
"Why don't you say something?"
Mom wrote on a piece of paper
he handed to me when she died.

I took that scrap as his penance.
By instinct, Dad understood his cows,
knew when one needed a kind word
to boost her spirits, but it took

a sharp slap with that note
for him to see that people with their smarts
aren't much different.

The farm wife receives a certified letter

It's from an Esquire in Chicago.
"Sincerely yours," he tells me,

but I see between the lines
how he wants to raze the barn

and turn over the garden for good.
The trees where my daughters played

house in the branches would vanish.
The creek where cows grazed

would be drainage. Behind his desk
this man expands the production

of boxed-up piglets who never own
a waking hour to wallow in sunlight.

My terse Grandma Iva was wise
as a serpent and innocent as a dove.

I know what she would write:
What you do is what you become.

Oddities

The farm wife defends her unlocked doors

I'd like to see who's itching for a twenty-inch
TV screen without a remote.

I don't own jewelry, not even a wedding band,
and anyone who squeezes the old piano

out the door can have it. We can sing a cappella
with the pitch pipe we never need to tune.

We don't keep guns because Jesus said,
"Turn the other cheek."

And we don't go for computers because
why complicate what we try to keep simple?

"Lock up for safety," my sisters say,
but Shep barks when strangers pull in.

Besides, locked doors make people more afraid.
They can't leave or be at home without

turning a deadbolt. Mom and Dad never slept
behind a barred door, but now they're tucked

inside vaults, as if the earth were a thief.

The farm wife explains why she doesn't mow her ditch

This is where Queen Anne pricked her finger—see
the center speck? Red to dark purple, almost black?
That was no accident. No one makes lace with a needle.
Grandma Iva's shuttle, shaped like a fish, tatted

chains of tiny knots that blossomed into doilies
until a Mennonite bishop rebuked her for vanity.
I suspect Anne was getting old and wished for some
bit of herself to be remembered. If that's vanity,

then who isn't vain? Our neighbor claims it's nicer
for a roadside to be mowed. He wants to be remembered
for straight rows and the absence of weeds. His headstone
already reads: "Gone to a Better Place." When I kick

the bucket, don't bother mowing my plot. Mark it
with chicory and lace and milkweed for the monarchs.

The farm wife directs visitors to the Skunk Lady of Howe

At Riverside Cemetery follow the hand-painted signs
till you reach a back-row boulder with a plaque

and two ceramic skunks. Downhill in the poison ivy,
Christina Sullivan lived in a dirt-floor shack.

On Sunday afternoons, Grandma Iva took Mom along
to bring Crissie a loaf of homemade bread.

After brushing cats off the chairs, they sat at a plywood table.
"Like playing make-believe," Mom said.

Crissie took a bite and fed the next to a friend.
Pigeons flew in to peck the crumbs and nest in the straw

of her bed. No one invited Crissie to church
because she smelled so bad. But her skunks never stunk.

It was Crissie who didn't take a bath.
She's like that saint who carried birds on his shoulders.

I wish I could have seen her do an Irish jig as she sang
"Charlie Over the River" with skunks on her shoulders

and a crow on her head. She was happy as a lark, Mom said,
till the men of Howe burned her shack and tied her skunks

in bags bound for the river. They built her a house
with a floor she could mop and glass in the windows.

Their wives soaped her up good, combed out the knots
in her hair while she cried. A month later, Crissie died

of cleanliness. I could pray to a saint like that.

The farm wife speaks of a standing stone

It's the biggest fieldstone in the county—
a slab of granite, pink as a sore thumb.

You can read on the cleft surface
how militia *escorted*

Potowatomi farmers to Kansas
and then how *Shup-she-wah-no*

turned around and walked the Trail
of Death back to his former life,

traveling by night till he reached
the shoreline where his razed village

had stood. He hid in the marshes
among whippoorwills and water snakes,

fieldstones stacked with his ancestors'
plowed up bones. White farmers

named our town for him, and our kids
are the Westview Warriors.

No one knows where the chief
lies buried. He could be in the bank

where Buck Creek borders
our back forty—where Dad slept

on humid nights in August,
lucky buckeye in his pocket,

one ear to the ground.

The farm wife discovers the giant rattlesnake of LaGrange County

I thought it was a monster farm wives concocted
to keep daughters from wandering too far

into a cornfield. Mom never could name
the Amish woman baffled by *an awful big tree trunk*

blocking the road. Before she could raise an axe,
that sycamore knocked her to her knees

and slithered into the corn. Any snake
you imagine is scarier than one you see,

but Mom swore this one had thirty rattles
and eyes red as signals at a railroad crossing.

Now that Mom's gone, I'm reading her diaries
and recognizing the rattle of a farm wife's

afflictions: *awful* cold today, *awful* hot,
awful ache in my left hip. As if a curse

had stung her days and nights. As if
God had given her a sweet tooth for cake.

Then said, "Let her eat dust with the snake."

The farm wife recollects the aftermath

After we rebuilt what the tornado
tore apart, Sam Hooley invited the neighbors

to see slides of straw poking through
plate glass and his own cow looking down

from the roof of Jay's Standard Station.
We met every five years to see the eggs

that flew to Michigan without a crack.
"That's my best butter dish," Martha cried

each time we spied what was left
inside the bank. Only when we moved

to the yard and the young fell asleep
in our arms, did we speak of the newlyweds

wrapped in chicken wire and Mattie Graber
at her own door, pulling against the wind.

Night eclipsed our faces as we lingered, peeling
apples in long spirals and passing the slices.

The farm wife carries a buckeye in her purse

It holds its luster
like the old, rubbed wood
of a church bench

but it's from Buck Creek
that drains our fields
and joins Pigeon River.

Dad carried one too
and his dad before him—
"to ward off rheumatism."

Pressing this one
to my palm, Dad returned
his to a pocket packed

with peppermints, odd nails,
and a few fortunes
from the Golden Buddha

on State Road 9 in Howe.
Dad was a deacon,
but he knocked on wood,

wished on bones,
and rubbed his buckeye
like a worry stone.

Tell me, if you know,
how else a farmer prays
without ceasing.

The farm wife drives past the buggies at BJ's Burritos

"More of the Hollywood Amish
or NRA—Not Really Amish,"

people in Shipshewana snicker, but it's us
Mennonites who put their barns

on postcards and drape their star
quilts in showroom windows. Because

farmland is scarce, Amish take
shifts at the Coachmen factory and move

to plain-featured houses in Village Farms—
colonials that hide the horse barn.

My friend Freida Schrock likes rolling out
her pie crusts on the granite top island,

but she's caught in a covenant
that makes clotheslines illegal.

She hangs laundry for a family of nine
in the basement where songbirds

never sing and the sun never shines.

Tidal Chart

The farm wife recalls the shadows of great ships

My daughters played house
in the orchard behind the barn,
spooning invisible cake
to dolls made of cornhusk

and twine. When did branches rise
like lighthouse stairs?
When did my girls spy
flags of ships crossing the horizon?

I must have been asleep
when they slipped away
on a humid summer night—
barefoot, long hair tangled.

Their combs lay side by side
on the bureau, burnished
strands knotted in the teeth,
and I remember

the wind like a serpent
rippling through green leaves,
promising things I could hold
but never keep.

The farm wife ruminates on cows

If I'd been born a fortune teller,
I'd read my family's future
in the black peninsulas of Holsteins. I'd see
my grandmother, an orphan growing up,
rub her hands on December mornings
in steam where they had lain.

The only dream my mother ever told
was how she drew away the baby quilt
and saw the snout, the full-moon eyes.
Pregnant, I would dream of joining them
in the fields, our bodies, heavy pears, pulling
branches to the ground.

My girls believe they're named for Bible women,
but each was named for a favorite cow,
a blessing of sorts, the only kind I knew, so that
even if they never have cattle in their barns
or live near fields in which they graze
they will have one guardian with a steadfast shape.

The farm wife remembers the funerals she presided over

While Dad hitched the trailer,
I'd lead my sisters to the special pen
and say, "Dearly beloved,
we are gathered to bless this calf
before he goes to market."

We each said something pleasant
about his brown eyes
and thick lashes,
his earnest tongue licking our hands.

By the time they started school,
my sisters threw their kisses
like passengers aboard a ship.

One chilly day, even a stick
of chewing gum
couldn't bribe them to the barn.

I poured the extra measure
of grain into the bin,
then stood alone with my Bible,
looking into soft eyes
that had never seen or blinked at evil.
For the last time I sang
"Children of the Heavenly Father."

It was snowing when I left.

The wind blew flakes into my face
and stung my eyes.

The farm wife balances the ledger before she goes to bed

Three hundred gallons of milk
      leak into the empty diesel tank.

A dozen brooding hens flap
      against the bars of their column.

Even the sheep I count leap
      into the Blue Lake beans.

So much to keep straight—
      like Uno cards in a losing hand.

How did the names of bovine ladies
      shrink into numbers to subtract?

How can I fall asleep
      with a bottom line that roars

like a combine's cutter bar
      crunching what it meets?

The farm wife shields the yellow jackets that stung her

Pete thinks we should pour gasoline
where they've burrowed near the fence post,
but winter frost will kill them soon enough,

all but the future queen, who will find
another cranny for her nest. "That's the problem,"
Pete says. "She might move in under the porch

or behind a shingle." I don't deny it hurt
when yellow jackets stung my arms and nose
and clung like burrs to my socks,

but those feisty wasps were fighting
for what they fear they will lose—
and who am I to fault them for that?

The farm wife looks out her window and shudders

It's ugly as sin, this aluminum centipede,
    where sycamores formed an island

and fencerow maples, bluish in the distance,
    made a breaking wave.

That surf kept me cool in August—
    half-submerged in dishwater or steam

that fogs the window when I'm canning. Cows
    in search of shade must miss that

fencerow most. Or tree swallows swooping
    over corn to snatch up bugs. Even winter's

wind in the eaves won't let me forget
    what neighbors cleared for the creep of sprinklers.

The north wind moans like homeless Job
    or Jonah swallowed by the whale.

The farm wife sells her cows

The cats gather by my kitchen door,
rubbing ribs against a box of overshoes
and spewing curses that waver
like an organ's vibrato. I've given them
every left-over in the fridge—none of it
seems to soothe them, though when we enter
the parlor where a sour scent still lingers
they hush and assume places, calico
sphinxes against the wall.

I switch on the radio, wait for
the first ones to lumber through—black
and white boulders—larger than you'd imagine
watching them in the field. If only
we could call them back, but by now
they must be past the beltway of Indianapolis,
peering through slats with eyes bewildered
as on the day we pulled them from their mothers.

The farm wife is adrift without her cows

Heifers breaking into sweet corn
kept me on my toes, dashing out

and back before the pots boiled over.
On frisky nights in spring, grown-up

jokesters bumped our bedroom wall.
When we rushed outside

they turned on cue to moon us.
They hardly ever trotted down the road,

but when they did, it gave me
an exciting story for sewing circle.

In forty years we never strayed further
than a week at Curtis Lake,

so when I went to say good bye,
all the ladies in the field

staggered up and gathered around me
tighter and tighter—like they knew

we were on a tiny island and the tide
was coming in.

The farm wife dreams of an afterlife in Sarasota

We wake at five to milk the cows,
but Pete buries his face deeper

in his pillow while I pinch the wilted
blooms of striped petunias too big

for their pots. Inside our trailer's knee-high
picket fence, there are chickens

with whirligig wings, a cross-eyed frog,
his and *her* plywood pigs. *I'm in heaven,*

I write on postcards of the ocean,
but I can't find the stamps. Every evening

we play shuffleboard with the Amish
in our court and then stay up late

watching repeats of *Bonanza.* We prefer
the first episodes with Adam.

The Cartwrights are rough in those,
but it's because they love the land.

I wake up when the rooster
we butchered last Easter crows.

The farm wife muses upon her Miracle Tree

Everyone laughed
when it arrived in a legal-sized
envelope and I showed them

the ad: "For 19.99, watch it
reach your roofline in a year."
Just as that stick, plain

as a toothpick, unfurled a leaf
Pete clipped it
with the mower. *That's it,*

I thought, but it grew back
above the red petunias
I added round its base.

We could use a miracle here,
with the cows gone
and the farm in reverse

mortgage. But when it
spouted slender branches
with narrow leaves

even the Schwan Man
who measured each week
lost interest. I ponder

the name *Salix babylonica*
and how merchants
traded sprigs of those trees

along the Silk Road. *Already
it weeps like a woman,*
I write in my diary. *Already*

*my neighbors dismiss it
as a dirty tree.*

Pastimes

The farm wife and her family sing a cappella

Four or five to a book and all of us
in bifocals, we edge close
to sing Mom's favorite hymn,
"O Perfect Love."

"No, it was 'Bringing in the Sheaves,'"
says my sister Neva, who can't agree
with me even on the weather. "After that,
214—'O Sacred Head Now Wounded,'"

says Eve, who prefers what slants
toward a dark loft. My cousin tosses us
the starting notes, then holds them down
as we scramble to our places.

Years ago, Grandma Iva held
the pitch pipe and we craned between
aunts and uncles to see the words.
Before we could read, we harmonized,

stepping out on the chorus of "Trust
and Obey." "Let's try that again
and pick up the tempo," says my sister
Pauline, who doesn't like any song

to drag. With Pete gone, she jumps down
to help the men on tenor then soars
to finish the last note—all of us balancing
on the cord of our breath.

The farm wife gives a eulogy for Pete

After we sold the cows and rented our fields,
Pete was supposed to slow down.
Instead, he worked full-time at Topeka
Seed & Stove, lifting as much as the young men
and driving a delivery truck on days off.
At home, he answered the call to fix
what was broken at the church.
It took food on the table or a rerun
of *The Waltons* to lure him to a chair.

But he did always honor the Lord's Day,
except for chores and teaching
Sunday school. After we walked our Sunday
company to their cars, we'd linger
to swing on the wooden two-seater
Pete rigged up near the rusty iron pump.

We'd hold hands and sing,
Tell my why the stars do shine,
Tell me why the ivy twines . . .

Or the song that's slightly naughty:
There once was a farmer who took a young miss
in back of the barn where he gave her a —
lecture on horses and chickens and eggs,
and told her that she had such beautiful—
manners. . . .

It was the best time of the week.

After the cows were sold and it was us
and Shep the Fourth,
we'd stay outdoors a long time,
watching darkness creep across
the field Pete had plowed and planted
and harvested, season after season,
row after row.

Sometimes we talked or sang,
but it felt good
to keep company with silence.

It was nothing we feared.

The farm wife endorses the game of Rook

"It's a mystery to me," I said to Pete,
"why I am dealt the Rook so often."
He thought it was due to my soft spot
for any bird dressed in black.

Even the bishop who said face cards
encouraged pride with their kings,
queens, and jacks, gave his blessing
to the plain-feathered Rook

and played it high. In our youth
Pete and I hosted wild tournaments
on Friday nights till midnight. We women
watched each other's faces

to decide what trump to call, while men
started bids at 140 and tried to shoot
the moon or con us into going set.
Perched upon a lap, our daughters learned

their colors from the cards, how to add,
subtract, and take a chance on the kitty.
Later, they taught boyfriends from college
the rules before introducing them to us.

But those days of Rook with horse necks
and Yoder Popcorn have flown. Now
they vote for Euchre or Crowns and order
carry-out pizza from East of Chicago.

The grandkids bring monster cards I can't
make heads or tails of. When it was me
and Pete, we played Rook low with a dead-hand
partner. It doesn't matter who wins, I said

when that random stack laid the cards
I needed. It's the fun of picking up the kitty
and feeling the bird nest inside your hand.
I saw on TV how rooks live like dukes

at the Tower of London and as long
as they do, the kingdom is safe.

The farm wife lingers in the root cellar

Pete would send the youngest grandchild
down to fetch a jar of carrots or green beans
or pull an onion from the bin. He didn't
suspect how I love to sit in dim light

amid the gleam of mason glass. Outside,
snow lies three feet deep, but here summer
is stacked to the beams and mummified
in potatoes. If I were an Egyptian queen,

I'd shun the plain, gray stones in Yoder
Cemetery. Bury me in a root cellar, I'd say,
with garlands of garlic and chili peppers,
among gems of peach and plum and cherry.

The farm wife launches the paratroopers

As a boy, Grandpa Milt made pocket
money pulling milkweed for farmers
taxed by the number in their fields.

He carted them in wagonloads—
stalks of green pods soft as old slippers.
In World War II, Dad picked ripe ones

for life preservers—twenty cents a bag.
They crackled like the crinoline
inside my cedar chest. It hurts to see

milkweed mowed down to make a tidy
ditch. Watch me send the parachutes across
this open field—an act of treason,

but once before I die, I'd like to see whirling
monarchs so thick they block the sun.

The farm wife salvages rags from her empty nest

My stitches pucker pods
cut from a green maternity dress

and halo the hollyhocks, taffeta
from a loose elastic slip.

Lacy baby socks make daisies
basted to broken zippers. Pulled

from the ragbag, Eve's flannel shirt
nibbles a tweed carrot and twitches

its coral button nose recouped
from Ruth's favorite cardigan.

To the washed-out blue
of Pete's handkerchief is tacked

the yellow satin of Sarah's prom dress.
Let it shine, let it shine

for this grandchild in my lap,
too young to make sense

of the preacher's salvation sermon,
but old enough to see in my book

how love comes back.

The farm wife looks up at the cosmos

When it's too nice to nap indoors, I take
an old knotted comforter to the back edge
of the garden, near tomato leaves I crush
for a last whiff of summer. Crickets chorus
round me and the combine's racket turns
to a purr the barn cats pick up, settling
near my head. It's then I look up at the cosmos,
struck by their petals, mandarin orange
against blue sky. The underside shines
radiant as monarch wings or the stained glass
of sun through tissue paper. Resting
by County Road N 400 W, I forget
laundry on the line, supper to fix.
For hours I've been napping. Now I am awake.

Travel

The farm wife goes to another reunion

I remember when we played wild rounds of Dutch Blitz
till milking time. But now no one owns a cow,

the young rarely come, and when they do, they leave
after lunch. This year we gather at a state park

in Indianapolis. Instead of dealing cards, cousins pass
cell phones with photographs and talk about gall stones

and Uncle Ervie's glass eye. Half asleep, I wander off
toward the Nature Center that displays a mastodon tooth

and a gray bird with eyes ringed in red. The notecard
says he's a passenger pigeon. He traveled with others

in clouds so thick they'd darken the sky and make a ruckus
loud as Niagara Falls. When their flocks were shot to pieces,

the scattered birds didn't have a clue how to live alone.
The last one, Martha, died in the Cincinnati Zoo. Maybe

I'll see her at next year's reunion.

The farm wife inspects her cedar chest

Common sense would rule against
the cargo I keep inside its hold:
a wedding dress that will never fit again,
baby shoes that jingle, dried flowers
no amount of water will ever bring back.

Unlikely provisions for such a long voyage
when one day I haul up the anchor
and let the current take me where it will.

The farm wife describes her Mystery Trips

Once or twice a year, I board a bus with strangers,
none of us knowing where we'll be
until we get there. It's like floating in meringue
with no notion of what's below.

I send everyone back home a postcard: the mouth
of Mammoth Cave, dunes that rise like pyramids,
the world's largest egg. My sisters think it odd
I never plan for Italy or a Caribbean cruise.

As girls, they studied maps, plotted their escape
from floors they could never scrub clean and sheets
that smelled faintly of what's bedded down in straw.
I travel the way of starlings, clustered

like a cloud that cracks the whip and then lengthens
into a river, leaving and returning, never asking why.

The farm wife visits the Levi and Catharine Coffin House

From the outside, it's plain and simple,
but, inside, each room has two ways

in and out and there are secret places—
a kitchen below Catharine's kitchen,

a basement with a spring-fed well.
Behind the headboard of the bed

is a door to a hiding place in the attic.
The Coffins heard shouting in the street,

but torches in the night couldn't give
those Quakers pause. They broke bread

with a hundred freedom seekers each year
and rubbed their shackled, frostbit feet.

We kneel to wash feet at our church too,
but they're already clean and seldom sore.

Last night I dreamed the house was much
too little. I knew I'd need to move

until I found a door that opened
into an empty room I forgot was there.

Today I'm clearing out the boxes in the attic
and then I'll begin on what's stored

in the coal bin and the barn. Whether or not
anyone needing shelter comes to my door,

it's a relief to know I have the space inside.

The farm wife sees the Promised Land

Our guide said *loblolly* is an old word for *gruel*—
that's what pioneers thought of as they fought

mud that stuck to wagon wheels. But for us
Loblolly Marsh Preserve was like walking through

the sea that Moses parted—stalks of prairie dock
on either side, spouting yellow flowers. Farmers

with a steam-powered dredge drained the land
a hundred years ago, but plagued by floods,

they finally let it go—let it go back to turkey-foot
and bristle grass, blue chicory, partridge pea,

and milkweed. I can't recall all those tribes
our guide could name. It's as if the wild ditches

I loved were told to multiply and make themselves
a nation. At the trail's end, we stood on a hilltop,

looking at the bulrushes in mudflats. I wanted
to run down, to see more wonders, more

and more, till I was lost in the Big Bluestem—
where roots stretch deeper than the height of men.

The farm wife reviews the Tornado Theater
at Menno-Hof Museum

It's the size of a large elevator, where kerosene lights
flicker, the wood floor shakes, and a whir of wind

clatters like my vacuum with a broken belt. It sweeps
me back to that humid Palm Sunday when our barn's

western side sweated like a hard-ridden horse
and bottle flies clung to the kitchen screen. Dad's cows

lowered their bodies to the ground and staggered up again.
"It's snowing!" my sister Neva shrieked when bits of paper

fluttered down. On the screen, the same green cloud
reaches for us with its outstretched finger—I squeeze

my grandkids' hands and close my eyes. That funnel veered
at Buck Creek and shot due east to Yoder Cemetery,

scooping up headstones, tossing them like dice.
"A miracle," Mom said, but it barreled on to crush

a trailer court and homes near Rainbow Lake.
In the rubble of Eli Yoder's house

all they found intact was a glass jug
with a carving stuck inside: "Fear God"

on one side— "God Is Love" on the other.
Eli took that as a sign of the Almighty's power,

but I believe whirling wind spins the bottle
and God is in the dark with us,

not writing down what happens next.

The farm wife finds grace in her empty barn

Inside the house, dust is dust,
but here it looks holy, suspended

in slanted light that slips between
boards. Jacob's ladder could be

rungs to a loft where barn swallows
brush the dark with the curve

of their wings. Every joint is pegged
tight as Noah's ark, but there's room

for everyone—nesting sparrows
and mice that scatter from burlap sacks.

When I slide the big door back,
sunlight rushes in to fill the empty bin

where Jesus could be reaching up
to touch black and white faces

gazing down. I like to picture him
swaddled by the breath of cows.

The farm wife collects frequent flyer miles

I find my seat on a gray plank
        and grasp stout rope tied
to a sycamore branch. Leaning back,
           I pump till I'm lifting off

over barbed wire, dusty beans,
        six-foot corn, my legs stretched
to spin the rusty rooster's arrow.
           I reach for what I see

and what I don't—The wind in my face
        whispers, *Esther, Esther,*
or is it you, my heart, pumping
           as I pump that speaks? "I'm here,"

I say, like faithful Samuel
        answered in the darkness.
Leaning into the arms of this world
           that push me forward, I forget

stiff arthritis and varicose veins.
        I let go of the back and forth
of brooms and mops, sweepers and irons
           and rock with the bliss

a rocking chair rocks or a pendulum
        swinging from the sun.

Acknowledgments

Although the farm wife is a fictional character, many of her stories harken back to stories from my family tree. I peeled, sliced, and simmered these accounts, adding this and that, till they turned into something new, like the fruit preserves in the farm wife's larder. I am therefore indebted to my extended family, the dead and living, for the harvest I gathered to fashion these poems.

I want to particularly thank family members who answered my questions about family history and farm life. Thank you, Mom and Dad (Mary and Gerald Miller), Aunt Marty (Bender), and Cousin Jan (Schwartz). Most of all, thank you, Aunt Doris (Mast). From your generous branches, I have plucked a bushel of anecdotes and stories. This book could not have been written without you and Uncle Bill and the farm you tended with such great love and care.

I would also like to express my gratitude to those who provided literary advice as I worked on *The Farm Wife's Almanac*. These folks include the poets in my monthly poetry group— Wendy Jones, Karen Kovacik, Elizabeth Krajeck, Bonnie Maurer, Gaye McKenney, Nancy Pulley, and Catherine Swanson; the members of my Mennonite writers group—Wilma Bailey, Jay Brubaker, Dan Hess, Martha Maust, and Jeanne Smucker; and my fellow colleague at the Indiana Writers Center, Kyle Craig. I am also deeply grateful for suggestions offered by Cascadia's DreamSeeker Poetry Series editor, Jeff Gundy, and the poets in my family: my husband, Chuck Wagner, and daughters ,Vienna Bottomley and Iona Wagner.

My deep appreciation also extends to artist John J. Domont, www.domontstudio.com, who kindly provided permission to use his painting, "Full Moon Winter Haiku," on the cover of this book.

Furthermore, I would like to thank the editors of the following magazines and anthologies where poems in this book, or their earlier versions, first appeared:

Black Warrior Review: "The farm wife tells the story of an aunt who planted trees" (earlier version appeared as "The Farm Wife")

The Center for Mennonite Writing: "The farm wife sings to the snake in her garden," "The farm wife lingers in the root cellar," "The farm wife and her family sing a cappella" (earlier version appeared as "The Acrobats"), "The farm wife reveals her recipe for letters" (earlier version appeared as "The farm wife speaks of letters"), "The farm wife looks out her window and shudders" (earlier version appeared as "The farm wife looks out her kitchen window")

The Christian Century: "The farm wife finds her necklace in the junk drawer," "The farm wife eats out at Marner's Six Mile Café," "The farm wife examines her Mennonite roots," "The farm wife muses upon her Miracle Tree," "The farm wife hoists the family flag," "The farm wife repeats a lullaby," "The farm wife looks up at the cosmos," "The farm wife shares her view on windows in the new sanctuary," and "The farm wife collects frequent flyer miles"

DreamSeeker Magazine: "The farm wife describes her Mystery Trips"

Flying Island: "The farm wife dreams of an afterlife in Sarasota" (earlier version appeared as "The farm wife moves to town"), "The farm wife ponders her mother's cookbook," "The farm wife describes meeting her husband at a walk-a-mile—a Mennonite dating game," and "The farm wife remembers the funerals she presided over." *Flying Island* nominated the latter three poems for a 2017 Pushcart Prize.

Friends of the Limberlost: "The farm wife sees the Promised Land"

From the Edge of the Prairie: "The farm wife recounts a close call," "The farm wife posts on her fridge," "The farm wife makes her Christmas list," and "The farm wife predicts the weather"

Hopewell Review: "The farm wife sees the shadows of great ships"

JuxtaProse: "The farm wife marvels at her mother's ordered house"

The Mennonite: "The farm wife sells her cows" and "The farm wife cites Proverbs 31:17—'She girds her loins with strength and makes her arms strong'" (earlier version appeared as "Inheritance")

Midland Review: "The farm wife ruminates on cows"

Public Pool: "The farm wife discovers the giant rattlesnake of LaGrange County" (earlier version appeared as "The farm wife meets the giant rattlesnake of LaGrange County"), "The farm wife balances the ledger before she goes to bed," and "The farm wife shields the yellow jackets that stung her"

Shenandoah: "The farm wife turns off the TV evangelist" and "The farm wife goes to another reunion"

So It Goes: The Literary Journal of the Kurt Vonnegut Memorial Library: "The farm wife explains why she doesn't mow her ditch" and "The farm wife defends her unlocked doors"

The Wabash Watershed: "The farm wife recollects the aftermath" (Second Place in Indiana Poetry Awards, rural category, "The farm wife speaks of the aftermath") and "The farm wife carries a buckeye in her purse" (earlier version appeared as "The farm wife speaks of her lucky buckeye")

The Writer's Almanac: "The farm wife sells her cows" (reprint)

Writers Resist: Hoosier Writers Unite (Chatter House Press, 2017): "The farm wife visits the Levi and Catharine Coffin House"

Undocumented: Great Lakes Poets Laureate on Social Justice (Michigan State University Press, 2019): "The farm wife receives a certified letter"

"The farm wife ruminates on cows" and "The farm wife sells her cows" appeared in *Evening Chore* (Cascadia/DreamSeeker Books, 2005), as did earlier versions of "The farm wife tells the story of an aunt who planted trees" ("The Farmer's Wife"), "The farm wife inspects her cedar chest" ("Cedar Chest"), and "The farm wife cites Proverbs 31:17—'She girds her loins with strength and makes her arms strong'" ("Inheritance").

Finally, I wish to express my appreciation to the Indiana Arts Commission. Many of the poems in this book were written with the assistance of grants from the IAC, with support from the National Endowment for the Arts.

The Author

Credit: Rachel Greenberg

Indiana's fifth Poet Laureate (2016-2017), Shari Miller Wagner teaches for the Indiana Writers Center; Indiana University-Purdue University's Religion, Spirituality and the Arts Seminar; and Bethany Theological Seminary's graduate program in theopoetics and writing. Wagner is the author of two prior poetry collections: *The Harmonist at Nightfall: Poems of Indiana* (Bottom Dog Press, 2013) and *Evening Chore* (DreamSeeker Books, 2005).

Her nonfiction includes two books she wrote with her father, Gerald Miller: *A Hundred Camels: A Mission Doctor's Sojourn and Murder Trial in Somalia* and *Making the Rounds: Memoirs of a Small Town Doctor*. She is also editor of books that grew out of her writing workshops*: Returning: Stories from the Indianapolis Senior Center* and *Finding the Words: Stories and Poems of Women Veterans*.

Her poetry has appeared in *American Life in Poetry, The Writer's Almanac,* and in several anthologies, including *A Cappella: Mennonite Voices in Poetry* and *Undocumented: Great Lakes Poets Laureate on Social Justice*.

Wagner and her husband, Chuck, live in Westfield, Indiana, and are parents of two grown daughters. Visit Wagner's websites, www.throughthesycamores and www.shariwagnerpoet.com, for information about her workshops and readings.

CPSIA information can be obtained
at www.ICGtesting.com
Printed in the USA
FSHW011712040819
60695FS